Go for It. . . GIRL!! !

Theresa Crosby

Go for It. . . . GIRL!!!

Cover art and cover design by Sheryl Rhoades
sherylrhoades@gmail.com

Interior Book design by D. Bass

ISBN: 979-8-218-51773-1

DEDICATION

I would like to dedicate this book to all the women in my life who have seen me throughout every stage of my life. To the women who have been my rocks and to help pick up the pieces when I needed it the most. You know who you are, but one, most important, woman needs to be mentioned, my MOTHER. She is, and will always be, the wind beneath my wings.

Contents

Introduction:

If there was a MAGIC PILL that would allow you to suddenly know how to handle all things "GIRL" for, let's say, from the beautiful age of 12 until you are no longer a teenager … 20ish, would you take it? Of course you would!! I know I would.

There have been plenty of times I have rewritten my story and redid certain things. Okay, many of those things in my head, of course, and YES, I would have gone back and done them differently if I just would have had the tools and guidance to empower ME and also heal ME along the way.

There are so many things today that are quite different from when I was growing up! Technology is the biggest difference. I thought it was cool to be able to have an aqua green beeper to spell out HI or I LOVE U and carry it around on my belt buckle. I know you want to laugh! Go ahead, it's ok! I laugh too, thinking back. While kids today follow their most famous influencer on IG or TikTok, there are certain things that will always remain the same. Growing up a girl in our society can be confusing and, let's face it, downright difficult. There are so many things we are faced with, whether it be at school or at home, and managing all the changes that go on within our own bodies as well as the world around us.

Life in these formative years can be so fragile and can shape who you are and how you operate as an adult later on. Let's also remember it can be fun, exciting, and adventurous along the way. Not all parts are hard or scary.

So, beautiful ladies, if there was a pill that I could magically give to all of you, I would in a heartbeat. But part of the beauty in life is to learn and grow from every single circumstance that comes your way.

My goal is to share some of my growing up "Girl" stories and allow you to relate, know you're not alone, and give you the tools necessary so you can make better choices and decisions to always feel empowered, even if it means we need to help you heal.

I have tremendous insight and a bit of experience when it comes to growing up "Girl." I really hope this inspires you even after all the bumps and bruises you may face. I want you to have the confidence to just *Go for It, Girl!!!*

Chapter 1

One of Many First Days

<u>MY Story</u>: Here I am, 11 yrs old, one month shy of 12. Heading into junior high school in early September. God, I was so nervous. Yes, it was a different school, but more than that, this was a new beginning for me, a chance to be a different girl. You see, since kindergarten, at the ripe old age of five years old, I was completely teased and isolated in my elementary/grammar school. I wasn't exactly what you would call the picture of a cool kid. I was 50 lbs., give or take, overweight, standing about 5'5" in 5th grade, and still growing, I might add. I didn't have the normal body for the latest and coolest clothes, let alone finding something that fit. The torturous days of outdoor lunch time were full of isolation on good days and tremendous teasing on bad ones. I was so glad to be outta there!!! Wooh!

NEW ME!!! RIGHT?

New school, no one really knew me. But, let me let you in on a little secret, quite frankly I don't think I knew myself at this point either.

I had been through so much but knew so little. My parents divorced three years prior, I was still very isolated, but somehow, I had all the hope in the world to start something new. Be someone different than I was, even though my body was already not what the other girls around me looked like. I still felt like I had a fighting chance to fit in, to be that girl who made friends easily and got a taste of all there was and to be a part of the things around me. We all want to fit in, right? Well, I wanted so badly to start anew. I had a sense of excitement, although I was extremely nervous from all the unknown. I had high hopes for my new school and for my new identity, of course!

I can remember that day like it was yesterday. When I think back to that period, it feels like an eternity, but for some reason, that first day feels like I can literally go back and touch it. The energy, the emotion, all right there if I were to close my eyes. As I walked the perimeter of the school, I saw girls sitting on boys' laps, kissing each other, and not like you do with your grandmother!!! I felt so awkward around all these kids making out!!! Why aren't they getting in trouble? I was definitely not used to seeing any of this up close!!! There was another group fist bumping, as to make a pact to solidify newly found friendships for the upcoming school year. OMG!!! I was completely lost, so unsure of myself and what to do next. God, did I need that magic pill to forge ahead. A guide to SOMETHING on how to survive would have been nice.

As I made my way through the next three years of junior high, this was such a huge learning period and transition in my life.

Now, looking back, it didn't have to be ALL bad, and at times it wasn't, so that is why I want to share some of my experiences with you. These young teenage years can feel overwhelming at times, but I am here to tell you it can also be a time for you to learn the uniqueness of who you are and to never become small in the presence of obstacles. Let's face it, all of us go through it at some point in our young adult lives.

So, Let's do this. *Go For It Girl!!!*

How would we handle this scenario: (YES!! GET A PEN AND YOU CAN WRITE IN THE BACK OF THIS BOOK IF YOU WANT. . . WHAT IS THE BEST VERSION OF THIS SCENARIO OR A SCENARIO LIKE THIS YOU CAN RELATE TO?)

Pick a day: One that you felt vulnerable and describe how you felt. Did you become closed off, scared, or even paralyzed with fear? Has there ever been a time that you knew you wanted to handle things differently and just wasn't sure of yourself?

<u>And/Or:</u>

Share your thoughts anonymously at this web link: www. goforitgirls. com

Questions you may have asked yourself:

How do I find my confidence in a new situation?

How do I make new friends, or friends at all, for the first time?

I was so unsure of myself and everything around me. I was definitely nervous. All that self-doubt came creeping in. Remember, I didn't have much positive interaction from previous years!!! Can you relate? I am sure you can.

Just remember, the one thing that I learned from growing up "Girl" is that we all have insecurities, and we think no other girl has them. That, my beautiful girl, is furthest from the truth. So, on any FIRST DAY of ANYTHING, *Go for It, Girl!!* It's OK to just be YOU.

Chapter 2:

Who Am I? Understanding Yourself.

My Story: Ok,so, who am I? What do you believe and know about yourself? For one, I knew that I was the sister to a younger sibling, a daughter to my two sets of parents, and a kid living in the middle of Queens, NY. I was extremely tall for my age and, If I remember correctly, I was already 5'7" - 5'8" in 7th and 8th grade, probably topping off in the weight category or 170 lbs. - 180 lbs.

This is really all I knew about myself since I wasn't really aware of who I was or my place in the world just yet. I just knew the basic things that didn't really describe that girl inside of me!!! I was just trying to "GET THROUGH" junior high, remember?

What I didn't realize was that there was this girl who was compassionate and loving and had so much to give. Someone who would like to shine and feel appreciated by my peers and my family. Being heard by my teachers would have been nice as well, but I have to admit a lot of those times I made myself small. This happened more than I would like to admit, but it was because I didn't want to get noticed since I was insecure and afraid to speak up. It could be as simple as being part of a school play, getting picked for a project a teacher assigned to the class, or feeling like I truly belonged in the circle of my peers I considered friends.

I was also bullied tremendously!!! I was talked about and made fun of almost every single day again. It was definitely a challenge.

I have to tell you, that "MAGIC PILL" would have come in handy when I needed to find my confidence for sure. What I didn't realize at the time, and now having those "remember when" conversations, was that most of us felt that exact same way. The difference was that some girls were able to overcome their fears to an extent, while others hid it rather well.

So, in an effort to *Go for It, Girl!!!* I want you to stop and take a breath. Close your eyes and really feel who you are. Here is your opportunity to know that it's ok to sometimes be unsure of yourself, BUT you have to remember that what makes you, you is so very special. We are all here to make an impact in this world and it's ok to discover all the wonderful qualities that make you unique! Remember, with all the billions of people in this world, there is only ONE OF YOU.

You will have many obstacles, but know you are seen and heard. You are not alone. You are so important. If you have fears, my advice would be to confide in someone to let them in. Talk to a peer, a sibling, or believe it or not, one of your parents. They love you and have been through some of their own stuff as well as once being a kid, true story!!! Anyone you feel safe with is a good person to speak with.

So, who am I??? was the biggest question for me. Write down all that you know you are. Be bold and confident.

Is there something that people don't know about you that you would like them to know? Be brave and *Go for It, Girl!!!*

So, did you decide what you like about yourself? NO? I didn't either at that age. But take a while to really think about it. If you took that MAGIC PILL, what would you want it to give you? Maybe something you think you might not already have?

Confidence is what I would have wanted and feeling good in my own skin. I may have been bigger than the average kid my age, but that was definitely not WHO I WAS. I was a good person, someone who was a great listener, I was honest, I was trustworthy, all the qualities I am sure you possess as well. How you treat others around you is important. It shows the type of person you are and will grow up to be.

I know we live in a world where we are glued to our phones, looking at the latest TikTok videos with the "Bold Glamour" filters and we somehow forget that most of that isn't real. I know it can be fun, and curiosity can get us to just try it out. I for one am GUILTY!!! But, please make sure you realize that those computer-generated images are NOT what beautiful young girls like yourself really are or look like. Physical beauty is only skin deep, and not to sound 'cliche' but who you are as a person and how you show up every day for the world around you, and most importantly for yourself, is really what matters in the end.

So, you might be different then your peers. You might be taller, shorter, skinnier, heavier, have long hair, short hair, or be into things that you just can't relate to anyone around you. That is OK!!! You are unique! We all are. We all have different things about ourselves that no one else has. That's what makes YOU, YOU!!!

There are things going on in your life that I am sure are very unique to you. It can be hard growing up "GIRL." All the changes with puberty!!! Getting your period, recognizing your body, growing boobs!!! OR not!!! The emotions are real, and I hear you loud and clear.

What I want you to do is really take time to get to know yourself. Be selfish!!! Learn what you like and what you don't. Embrace your uniqueness while also embracing anything that you are not 100% confident about. Recognize that you are a beautiful human being, and this part of your life should also be fun and exciting.

Accept where you are in this exact moment. You are right where you need to be.

Accept all things YOU and be who you want to be. *Go for It, Girl!!!*

Building self-esteem and confidence.

I believe it's extremely important to surround yourself with others who you look up to. To also be with other girls who are not judgmental and have some goals and hobbies that are similar to yours. It's very important to have other women and girls around you that give you confidence and support. They should be fun to be around, as well as someone in whom you can confide.

There are a ton of support groups out there, but you can start your own! You can also always come in and join my clubhouse for support as well. You can find the website at: **www. goforitgirls. com**

Here at our clubhouse we will always talk about the real issues and have an open line of communication to express ourselves and have a safe place to accept all that you are, no matter what stage you are at.

So how do we build self-confidence? How do we build our self-esteem?

For me, it didn't happen overnight. I struggled tremendously with learning to just love me!!! Life is hard, right? School, fitting in, home life, making and keeping friends can just be so overwhelming at times.

Positive affirmations can be a good way to start:

- I am Confident
- I am Smart
- I am Lovable
- I am Worthy

You may not necessarily believe all these things at once but make it a routine every morning when you get out of bed to say these things to yourself, even if you don't yet believe them. You can also make a small sign to stick on your mirror in your bedroom or in the bathroom. It can be a great reminder to help put you in a positive mood to start your day off right.

Just remember, knowing who you are and who you want to be in this world can take time. Nothing happens overnight, but as long as you do some of these small things, I promise you will get to know yourself better and better every day, and hopefully so will the rest of the world!

Chapter 3

Who Doesn't Love Having Friendships?

Building Healthy Relationships:

How great is it to get invited to a birthday party for one of your friends? Or to go to concerts together, maybe see the latest movie. What about just hanging out after school at your house or theirs? Right? So much fun. You have lots of laughs, inside jokes, and maybe some stories that only you and your friends share. You can make TikTok videos together or share fun pictures on Instagram. The time together can be amazing!!! Everything's better when you have great friendships. Some of these friendships can last a lifetime or well into adulthood.

It can feel great to be a part of something. In general, being in a group with people who share your interests is a great way to experience the things around you. This is completely normal, as long as they are healthy and respectful.

Sometimes friendships can happen overnight. You make an instant connection with someone or a group of girls and suddenly you are getting invited to all their favorite activities. You start to identify with being in this group of girls. Why wouldn't you? You all like similar things, you seem to have the same fashion sense, you listen to cool music together, and might even have a group of boys who you hang out with from time to time.

Other times, friendships can take longer to develop. You might end up having to partner up at school on a project with someone you've never met. At first it can be uncomfortable and awkward. You don't think you have much in common with this person and then suddenly you find yourself laughing and joking with them, getting to know them little by little. You find out they, too, like some of the things you like and before you know it, you guys are hanging out together outside of school.

No matter how it happens, life with friends can really shape your experiences as you grow up Girl!!! The trick is to make sure that, no matter how you met your friends or who they are, you always still stay true to yourself first.

MY Story: As you all are aware, making friends for me did not come easy. My elementary school years were mostly spent isolated, so this friend thing was very new to me. Once entering this first year (7th grade), I knew a group of girls who you would call noticeably popular, well known, or at least part of a group that was considered cool. One by one these girls started to befriend me. I was getting invited to birthday parties, after school get-togethers and even weekend hangouts!!! I was over the moon excited. Who wouldn't be?

This artificially seemed to build some self-esteem and excitement. I enjoyed spending my days with these new girls. What I failed to realize back then is that I was basing how I felt about myself on the acceptance from others. This can be a dangerous way to create a rollercoaster ride for your self-esteem.

You see, some of these girls were not so nice all the time. They found ways to gossip, spread rumors, and use peer pressure to put some girls, me included, in situations that were extremely uncomfortable. It was sometimes as simple as going somewhere I knew my parents didn't know about, or trying things such as cigarettes (which currently would take the place of what you know as vaping) and/ or bringing boys around that probably didn't have the best intentions. It seemed cool at first, but somewhere in my gut these things felt off and weren't the kind of things I would ever think to do on my own.

Dealing with Peer Pressure:

This is when having some confidence comes in handy. You might be in certain situations that feel, to put it lightly,

"NOT RIGHT." You can absolutely speak up and not do something you don't want to do, even if the people that are putting you in these situations are who you consider friends. If you don't want to do something, just say NO. In the end, please know that if someone is truly your friend, they will understand. *Go for It, Girl!!!* Use your voice and be brave

Always, always know that you have a platform to express yourself. I have made sure that girls can come to the clubhouse and anonymously share how they feel and seek some advice. *Go For It, Girl Clubhouse!!!* You are invited.

I am in no way saying it's easy. When your friends are all having fun and you think it might be fun or ok to join in, please listen to your gut. Ask yourself if you would otherwise be engaging in this activity if your friends hadn't asked you to.

Listen, I have been that teenage girl who went off with their friends to a place maybe my parents didn't care for, or tried to smoke, or have that beer (didn't do that until I was in high school) and of course sometimes I got caught and sometimes I didn't. These things can be seemingly harmless at first glance, but there are some things that you can never undo.

I was that girl who ended up caught up in wanting to be so accepted and ultimately noticed that I found myself in a situation one afternoon with my so-called "friends" and a "BOY" who ultimately sexually abused me. There were things I did that day that I was peer pressured into. Things that would stay with me for years to come. Things that at the time made my phone ring with other girls harassing me and calling me names. Things to this day that would correlate to being completely bullied online. These things made me feel bad about myself. At the time, the thought of disappointing my friends seemed far worse than going through with what that boy made me do.

Ultimately, if I could go back in time and take that "MAGIC PILL" the courage would have been given to me to walk away and say "NO." I would want that courage to protect myself and to never let anyone force me into anything I didn't really want to do. I want to give that strength to you.

The only reason I am sharing this is so YOU can know you are not alone and that your decisions as a beautiful young girl can help how you manage "growing up girl!!!"

Don't get me wrong, I love, love, love girlfriends and friendships. They can be beautiful and so much fun. I just find that when you are trying to figure yourself out, who you are can become blurry. That's why I really think it's important to take some time and get to know yourself. Always feel safe to have a voice and say "NO" when you just don't want to do something that doesn't feel right to you.

Go for It, Girl!!!

Who doesn't love to have friends? I know I do!!! The friendships I have now are loving and loyal and trusting and understanding. You deserve that as well. You can have that at any age! Set your boundaries and decide to put yourself first. *Go for It, Girl!!!*

Chapter 4

Handling Emotions

How are you feeling? Honestly, sometimes I feel great, all together, and happy. Other times I feel lonely and sad and empty and agitated. It can be really rough to get a hold on what you are feeling externally as well as internally. Growing up a girl has us going through so many changes, both physically and emotionally.

By now, most of you are menstruating and with that comes an influx of hormones throughout every month. Great! The world says you're a "woman" now, but has anyone remembered to tell you it can come with bodily discomfort and a wave of emotions? So, how do you handle this along with all the day-to-day social interactions that are happening all around you? Now would be a great time to get a hold of that magic pill so you can navigate all this stuff!

I promise, I went through the exact same thing.

MY Story: I felt like I couldn't begin to tell my friends, let alone my parents, what I was feeling. Honestly, I didn't even know most of the time myself. I needed to break some feelings down and take a breath and feel okay. Some big things happened to me; you know the boy incident at the forefront of it all. I started to get harassed and teased at school, which just reminded me of how much I was made fun of and teased in elementary school. I wasn't sure who my friends were anymore. You see, even girls I thought were my friends started to make fun of me. This over-whelmed me and sent panic deep in my stomach. Oh no, what was happening? I was also being harassed at home from random people calling me names on the other end of the phone. Laughing and saying horrific things. The panic that set in!!! God forbid one of my parents ever picked up that phone.

At the time, it became harder and harder to handle school work. Math, science, global studies, language class, it all became so much harder and overwhelming. My world seemed to be caving in on me. I didn't have anyone to speak to about what happened to me and, somehow, I felt like it was all my fault. The guilt and bad feelings gave me a feeling of unworthiness. The shaming about my body was torturous, which led to so many physical insecurities. These insecurities got carried through to my high school years and was, sadly, a part of my identity for quite some time into young adulthood.

It wasn't until a couple of years later that I was able to reach out for support to a therapist who made me realize that NONE of it was my fault. It took a while to balance my emotions. I wish I would have had someone or somewhere to go to feel supported and not judged. It would have prevented so much unnecessary self-hate.

Here and now, I want a place like *Go for It, Girl Clubhouse!!!* to give you a safe space for self-love, to anonymously speak out, be heard, feel empowered, and heal.

Understanding and managing emotions:

Emotions can be a complicated thing. Sometimes it's because our bodies are doing its thing, which means you are absolutely NORMAL. You will begin to know what to expect during that time of month. You may want to just curl up on the couch, wear comfy clothes, watch a good movie or series on Netflix, eat yummy food, and shut the world out. That is so OK!!! We all have done it. But, if something ever happens to you that makes you feel a certain way, no matter how big or small, like it did to me, know you have a place to speak about it. You have a right to feel angry, upset, scared, and even confused. Sometimes, confiding in a friend who you absolutely trust can be great, but you also might need to speak to an adult you can trust as well. If these options don't seem possible for you, here is where I need you to absolutely know you are truly not alone.

There are resources out there you can go to in order to feel safe and heard. You are always welcome in our *Go For It, Girl Clubhouse!!!* Check it out if you'd like. My mission is to give each beautiful girl, like yourself, a place where you can be honest and tell your story.

Coping with stress and anxiety:

How we handle our stress and anxiety is extremely important to our mental wellbeing. There are healthy ways to do this. You can dive into activities you love in order to relieve some stress. Meditation might be unfamiliar to you, but you can start off simply either right before you go to bed or right before you start your day. Put some calming music on, close your eyes, and just take some deep breaths. Imagine a happy and beautiful place that you would love to go to and imagine yourself there. You can take 3 minutes, or 5 or 10 to just simply BE. For example, breathe in to the count of four, hold for four counts, breathe out to the count of four and repeat for as long as you need or want. This can help promote a feeling of calmness. Clear your mind of any negative thoughts and relax. This might feel weird at first, but I know it has helped me to start my day off positively or end my day clearing out any anxieties that have stressed me out.

Let's be honest. That was not always how I handled stress and anxiety and, as a matter of fact, I had some unhealthy ways of coping.

MY Story: Somewhere around the age of 15, during that first year of high school, I found myself with a boyfriend, obviously completely monitored by my parents. Although teenagers will always find ways to circumvent parental authority, I was no different than any of you.

We spent weekends together doing normal boyfriend and girlfriend things, like going to movies, parks, hanging out with groups of friends, going to concerts, and he was sometimes invited to my house for family dinners. Life felt fun and I finally felt NORMAL. My school studies were on track, no more being made fun of, or made to feel like an outcast. I had someone who cared about me and found me to be pretty. I was happy, or at least that's what I thought.

This young love was what you would consider normal. But what I failed to realize was how fragile I was during these years. I always survived or got through particular events or incidents in my life, but I never really understood how to cope with all the stress and anxiety, which quickly turned into depression.

When this relationship ended, I was hurt, stressed, anxious, and at the time, heartbroken. I didn't know how to cope, since I thought I couldn't possibly talk to my mom. (Although not true at all, we can get back to that at another time.) All my girlfriends had boyfriends and couldn't relate to what I was going through. As a result, I started having many negative feelings about myself. I felt unworthy, unlovable, sad, and lonely. All those feelings I had when I was in elementary school came rushing in. So, late one night when I couldn't take it anymore, I began to cut myself. I cut myself to alleviate the pain. The physical pain was no way near the emotional pain I was going through. But I cut really deep into my arm without realizing it, and the bleeding wouldn't stop. Oh no, now what? Panic was setting in as I realized I might need medical attention. Now I had no choice but to tell my mom!!! That meant waking her up and explaining what I just did. How do you really explain why you held an open sharp scissor to your arm as tears were flowing down your face? NOT from the physical pain, but from all the horrible feelings you had about yourself.

That night with my mom was long. She was terrified for me and did what any mom would do! She brought me right to the emergency room and of course, had me evaluated by a mental health professional to make sure her daughter would not try to hurt herself again! Or worse.

As the people in white coats bandaged me up, I saw glances from grown-ups who eventually made their way over to me to "discuss" and "evaluate" my current state of mind. Ha! Ha! Okay, I thought. PROTOCOL!!! They just had to do their job and ask all the questions about hurting myself and if I was going to do it again.

So what did I do? I answered every question the way I knew they would want me to. This would guarantee me they weren't going to have me stay in this cold hospital overnight or possibly longer for that matter. And that's when I realized, even at such a young age, that the system was BROKEN.

No professional sat me down and offered ways to feel better about myself or gave me tools that I could have used to not let myself get so overwhelmed, or an outlet that allowed me to know that I wasn't alone. I truly did not want to KILL myself. I just wanted to stop feeling so bad. I needed someone to ask me if I was okay.

Believe it or not, that drive home from the emergency room with my mom was the only time that evening I felt comforted. She told me how much she loved me and wanted me to be happy. I should have gone to her from the beginning, but when you're a teenager your world can seem like it's unrelatable. I knew I scared her that night, and I didn't want to add any more stress onto her. She had adult things going on and the last thing I needed was for her to have me under a microscope moving forward, so naturally, as the days and weeks went on, I pretended to feel better than I did. Eventually, I felt better, and life seemed to go back to normal.

I am sharing this time in my life to let you know that I have not always been able to handle my emotions on my own. Life can feel too big at times, but before you get to a place similar to where I was, know that there are people, peers, groups, and a bunch of resources that can help you sort out your feelings without any judgment.

I have those resources for you at the back of the book. Never feel alone and know you can reach out if you are in need.

There are so many different ways to handle our emotions. But having a place you feel safe to do so is so important. Unfortunately, there is no MAGIC PILL that could prevent you from having some pretty BIG emotions, but having BIG emotions especially for the first time is completely normal. You are not alone!

Chapter 5

Embracing Yourself and Your Uniqueness

How do you see yourself? Do you know how special and unique you are? Are you self-conscious or do you have self-confidence? There are so many changes we go through growing up "GIRL." We are constantly being shown images of "perfect" bodies, beautiful girls on social media, and on "reality" T. V. Our famous influencers seem downright perfect!! Most of the stuff we see, by the way, is filtered or airbrushed and pictures are taken a bunch of times to get just the right lighting or angle. I didn't have to worry about social media way back when, but this stuff still existed in magazines, and in Hollywood for sure.

MY Story: Let me tell you something,having confidence was not something I knew anything about. As a matter of fact, I was a whole half a foot taller than most of my peers my entire childhood! By the time I was in high school I had already reached my full height of 5'10" with my weight topping out at 225 lbs. Not exactly the ideal look for a young teenage girl. I felt so out of place, more like I should be trying out for the high school football team instead of the cheerleading squad or even a dance class. My confidence level was less than healthy. Anytime a new fashion trend came on the scene, I would absolutely cringe, hoping and praying that it would be something I could partake in. Thank God, my high school days were in the Grunge era, with baggy colorful pants and flannel shirts. Look it up! You might even laugh!

The teasing during my high school years was definitely far less than what it was in my prior years, but learning to love myself seemed nearly impossible. It was hard to understand that there was and is no such thing as perfect. I definitely failed to embrace all the wonderful things about my body that are so unique to me.

Yes, I was definitely taller than your average girl, but guess what?! Today when I walk in a room and want to make an entrance, it is not hard to get noticed. I was always really strong, which helped me later on to get into a healthy lifestyle with weightlifting that I really enjoyed and still do today. I also loved to sing. I joined the chorus and the gospel choir and for a short time found "MY VOICE."

Of course, the voice inside my head which always said I wasn't good enough crept in. I might not have appreciated that operatic voice that I once had but, looking back, I had solos during holiday school concerts, practiced many days with my chorus teacher, and should have learned to appreciate all the things that were unique to me.

Don't we all have some talents that are unique to us? Maybe you can draw, or you have a beautiful imagination to see things differently? Maybe you love to dance, do gymnastics, or have a knack for writing poetry. Maybe science is your thing and you love exploring all things about the universe and beyond. I want you to realize this is unique to you. You are special. I want you to have a voice… to *Go for It, Girl!!!* Be you!!!

Explore everything!

Write down what you think is special and unique about you or just take the time to acknowledge these things that you love and enjoy. If you have a talent or something you like about yourself, never be shy about it, or at least find ways to express it. You may never know what or where this can lead. These interests can also help you to explore and figure out what you want to do later on in life. Maybe you want to start your own business, become a sports coach, or design clothing. Your options are limitless.

Importance of self-care and self-love:

It's ok to be selfish, take care of yourself!!! Make sure that your needs are met by being true to yourself. Learning to love yourself can be difficult, trust me, I know firsthand. But when you give yourself what you need, it can be empowering. I know some of you are in the middle of trying to get into college and have been working hard studying, maybe you are in an after-school program, and just feel tired and overwhelmed. Speak up! Tell your parents how you feel. Maybe you just need a weekend to relax! Get your nails done and enjoy some downtime. Embrace something you find enjoyable. Listen to your favorite music or see if you can find something you would like to do that makes you feel good.

Self-care and self-love are sometimes overlooked and as a teenager your needs can sometimes be overlooked even by YOU. It's important to check in with yourself and make a mental note of how you are feeling. Adults are not the only ones that need to do this. As a matter of fact, if you start doing this early, it can help you when you enter the adult world. There's nothing wrong with knowing when you can go full steam ahead or when you need tranquility. It's all about balance, so *Go for It, Girl!!!*

Here are some things that I do, and have done in the past, to give myself the attention I need:

Salt caves, massage, float pods, getting my nails done, finding a nice walking or hiking trail, going by the beach, or just calling up a girlfriend and making some plans together for the day. There is no right or wrong when it comes down to self-care and self-love. Whatever it is that helps you to nourish your inner being is great. Just know it's TOTALLY okay to do so. It can be very refreshing.

Chapter 6

Dealing with Family Dynamics

Family can be wonderful. Who doesn't like family vacations, BBQs, moms and dads being there to take care of you when you're sick? Siblings to be with you when you need them and maybe confide in and hang out with from time to time.

OK, OK, families can be a lot more complicated than that. Your parents may still be together and sometimes you may have parents that are divorced. This can mean trying to balance time between both parents' schedules as well as your own. Let's also now throw in siblings that are younger or older than you, so everyone is basically going in different directions. Even if you are an only child, let's face it, you're a teenager with friends of your own, school work to take care of, and maybe even your own little job after school or on weekends. So, how do you balance it all? Family dynamics can be tricky to maneuver. I have experienced all of it and, at times, it wasn't easy.

MY Story: Shortly after my parents separated, my brother and I were splitting our time between both parents. Mom during the week for the most part and Dad worked on the weekends. After the initial shock and confusion of it all, it felt like this was our new norm. Little did I know that another piece of the puzzle was right around the corner. It began with the ringing of the phone!!! I answered, "Hello?" A man on the other end clearly said, "Hi, can I speak to your mom?" I was defensive and curious and asked who he was??? He said his name and I was so confused as to how this strange man knew my mother. Of course, being a moody preteen, I was just not having it at the time. I was angry and heartbroken over my parents' divorce, so I was going to make a statement and not let this man off easy. Who was this person? I wasn't about to be nice. Why should I, right? We already had a new routine, and no one was going to take more of my mother's attention!! All of a sudden, the phone call disconnected. I remember giggling and smirking as I took credit for the abrupt dropped call. Of course, my mother called him back and scolded me, but somehow, I felt like our entire family dynamics were about to shift yet again!

This man who became my stepfather later on did not have it easy! If he said blue, I said purple. I wouldn't dare listen to him at all. He wasn't my dad! But honestly, I wasn't exactly listening to my father either at that point. He, too, had a new person in his life, and I was angry as to where I fit in. Family situations can be tough. Sometimes they can feel like you don't have a place, or the place you have can make you feel like you go unnoticed. My brother is three years younger than I am, and during your preteen and teenage years that can seem like worlds apart. Needless to say, I wasn't talking to him about my feelings and most of my friends had parents that were together. Who could possibly understand what I was going through?

Not all situations end up badly. Eventually, the weekends with our dad gave us some quality time together. We were always doing activities, like going to our cousin's house on Long Island to play in the pool. We also went to different parks, went rollerblading in the summer and ice skating in the winter. My brother and I eventually inherited a new family from my dad when he married my stepmom. This largely contributed to more birthday celebrations and fun filled holidays! Memories I treasure until this day were largely from that time period.

It also turns out the man that became my stepfather was the kindest and most gentle man who I know and love today. We had our fights and battles for sure. But he always showed up for me as well as my mom and brother. He showed me what true dedication to an already made family looked like.

As a matter of fact, on my wedding day, both my dad and stepdad would walk me down the aisle hand in hand. So, what seemed like chaos at the time turned out to be a beautiful blessing in the end.

Communicating with Parents and Siblings:

Remember, school during this time was really hard for me. I didn't fit in most of the time, let alone handle my parents' divorce well. I want you to understand that no matter what your family dynamics are, you should always feel safe to speak up. You are an important part of your family, and everyone has feelings and emotions. Our parents are also human and sometimes get wrapped up in juggling their own things. If you are feeling upset about something that has happened to a parent or a sibling, say something. Sometimes communication is key! If, for some reason, you need to vent outside of that, you can post anonymously in the clubhouse. You will be surprised at how many other girls are going through the exact same thing!

Handling Family Conflict:

It would be silly to say that you will never come across conflict, but how you handle that conflict can make a world of difference. Remember, family doesn't always have to be a blood relative either. Families come in many different shapes and sizes. No matter what your FAMILY looks like, it is important to be respectful to each person. Communication is key and will allow us to resolve an issue that you otherwise thought was unfixable. Just like when we have misunderstandings with friends from time to time, the same is true with our families. Arguments are bound to happen when you have different personalities in a household, but you are part of that household, so *Go for It, Girl!!!* Speak up. If something is bothering you, more than not, your family would want to know about it. If you and a sibling are having issues, see if you can sit down and talk it out. Nothing is perfect. Trust me, my brother and I would fight quite a bit. Now, there is nothing that we wouldn't do for each other.

Every family has different rules that are unique to them! You might not always like those rules, but as a teenager, you need to find a way to follow them. Just like when you reach the phase of adulthood there are rules we must follow. There are conflicts that arise, but learning how to deal with difficult things in your own family can set you up for success later! Always *Go For It, Girl!!!* Be the best version of you for yourself and, of course, the people we call family!!!

Chapter 7

Digital Well Being

Navigating social media

We live in a world of technology and an array of different social media platforms where we can instantly scroll through hundreds of pictures that are of your friends or of your latest influencers. Following the newest trends can sometimes be fun, but not all are safe. It's important to make sure it is nothing that would put you in harm's way.

It's also important to realize that some of what you see on social media isn't exactly real or truthful. For example, there are many girls that post images of themselves that are through an array of different filters. On your phone alone, you can alter a picture to your liking and easily post it. Sometimes this can create a distorted version of someone and give you a negative view of yourself. We start to compare ourselves to other girls and feel bad about our bodies and what we look like. This can be very dangerous and can lead to all sorts of issues, like eating disorders, negative self-talk, low self-esteem, and even depression.

Now, I am not saying you should avoid social media by any means. In this day and age, we have access to so much information and the ability to connect with people all over the world. It's very fascinating how the world has changed. Just understand that not all content is "good" or "healthy" content.

So, when you find yourself following a person, ask yourself one very important question? How does it make you feel? If the answer is NOT GOOD, then just scroll on by. There is no reason to start judging yourself based on someone else you may not actually know! Or, even if it's someone you do know, remember this,you are so very special, you are so very unique, you are beautiful because you are you. No ONE single person is better than you. By now, my hope is that you have learned how to be a *Go for It, Girl!!!* So, stay confident and proud to be you. Enjoy social media and all it has to offer, but always stay true to yourself.

Online Safety and Cyberbullying

There is also another part of social media that we need to talk about, and that is your safety and cyberbullying. Let's talk safety first: remember, not everyone is truthful on the internet and social media platforms are one of the easiest ways to communicate with people, even if you don't know them personally. There is a term called "catfishing." This is when someone pretends on social media to be some-one different to trick a person and lure them in. This is always for bad intentions. They will use fake photos and lie about who they really are to get you to do something. This can put you in danger and you should never start talking to someone online who starts asking you personal questions and wants your information. If you are of dating age, always tell your parents and/or a friend who you are talking to. You should never plan to meet up with someone alone, especially if you haven't been able to truly verify who they are. Better to be safe than sorry. Your safety must always come first.

Now, on the topic of cyberbullying. This is something that has become increasingly more and more common over the last decade. Bullying in general can be extremely harmful, as I have experienced this firsthand. Cyberbullying, no matter if it's being done to you, or you are the one doing it, is wrong.

Many times, people say things online without ever thinking of how it can affect the other person receiving the message. We tend to hide behind the excuse that we can write whatever it is we may impulsively "think," without any consequences. The truth is, YOUR WORDS can have a HUGE impact on someone, both positively and negatively.

Growing up "Girl" can be difficult as it is. We are constantly being judged by our peers and we can feel the pressure to fit in, be liked, and feel like we belong. The last thing we need is to be ATTACKED on social media and made to feel ridiculed, made fun of, or, worse, Isolated.

It is important to be authentic and to have a voice. Your opinion always matters, but it should never be at the expense of someone else. Be kind and respectful of other girls. You may not always agree with another person, but our differences are what make us special. You can be a role model to someone who can relate to you. You can set an example to other girls around the world. You can have a kind word for someone who really needs it. You shouldn't ever participate in hurting someone's feelings, especially when everyone can see it. I always want you to *Go for It, Girl!!!* by setting a good example. And by speaking your mind and staying true to yourself. Positivity can be contagious, as can negativity. Always choose the former. You will shine!

If you find yourself being bullied online, it's imperative you let someone know. It should be someone that you trust, maybe a teacher, a coach, an older sibling, or your parents. There is always something that can be done to address the situation and you should never have to deal with it on your own. Don't let it escalate and get out of hand. I don't ever want you to feel bad about yourself because someone online who you may or may not know said something offensive or insulting. Remember, you can't control how someone else behaves, but you can make sure you remove yourself from the situation by turning off, unfollowing, or blocking a person who is making you uncomfortable. You can even go further by reporting them if necessary. I don't want you to ever suffer in silence.

I have built the *Go for It, Girl Clubhouse* for this reason: to empower and help heal you and to bring forth positive ideas and support for all girls. It's a place where there is NO JUDGMENT. A place to talk, have fun, and feel safe!

Now go have at it, in a magical age of connecting!!

If you have been the victim or know someone who has experienced this, I want to give you some resources that you can go to. I have listed them in the back of this book.

Chapter 8

Exploring Passions and Hobbies

Finding your interests and talents.

By now, there are things that you just love doing. You may even have talents that are unique to you. Have you been able to really explore them? Maybe you love cooking, or baking. Maybe you love designing things. In this day and age, the possibilities can be endless. You have the ability to create content online that is unique to you. You can make music and immediately put it up for the world to hear. Anything is possible.

You may not know what you really like or like doing. That's ok, too. The idea is to try things. Maybe it's as simple as trying out for the debate team one semester and finding out you have an incredible knack for public speaking. Or you decide to join a dance class and you realize a passion inside you that will allow you to one day open up your own studio. You never know where things like this can take you.

I know it can be scary or intimidating when you are first starting something. Maybe you have some self-doubt but, believe me, *Go for It, Girl!!!* Life is a true adventure, and your mind is a powerful tool. If you believe in yourself the world will open up to you and show you just how amazing you are.

MY Story: So, the one thing that I absolutely loved doing was SINGING. In elementary school it was mandatory to be in chorus. Well, for a while, I believed I was somewhat tone deaf. This was due to having some clogged ears from many childhood ear infections. So, by the time I was five and in first grade I was lined up for a routine ear, nose, and throat surgery. Once everything was done and I was recovered, I can for sure say, without a doubt, I found my voice. It was a loud, strong voice. I had a vocal range that you would call soprano and, oh boy, did I sing. Through many tough and isolated school years, I still landed many solos and while in high school I was also part of the gospel choir, where I spent a lot of time with my vocal teacher. She completely believed in me and offered me a chance for a scholarship to train operatically. Amazing, right? Well, not exactly. You see, I was extremely insecure and filled with self-doubt. What if I wasn't good enough? What if I couldn't really make it? I ended up talking myself out of something that could have led to something great. A missed opportunity that might have taken me in a direction I never even knew existed, and all because I didn't believe in myself. I am telling you this so you don't make the same mistake as I did. I didn't have anyone really telling me to reach for the stars and dream big. Not that my parents wouldn't have supported me if I pursued this, but my lack of self-confidence led me to silence my own voice.

I wish I had that little MAGIC PILL once again to know I was the captain steering my own ship, that I was powerful and could Go for It, Girl!! Life can be filled with twists and turns and taking chances. Take that chance, there is NO WRONG path. It may lead you to a life that is all about your passion. When you are fulfilling your passion, you are living your best life!!!

Pursuing your dreams and goals

When you were a little girl, I am sure you would sit and daydream. Maybe you dreamed about what you want to be when you grow up! Maybe you wanted to become a princess in a beautiful castle, maybe when you got a little older you wanted to be a police officer, helping to make the world a safer place. Maybe now you want to be a professional traveler, developing content for the world to see! The point is, every single dream you had and have is real, no matter how crazy someone else thinks it is! You never have to minimize those dreams to accommodate another person's opinions or thoughts. *Go for It, Girl!!!* Dream big, and let life unfold for you.

Now, I am not saying everything will just come easy as long as you dream. You will have to set some goals for yourself along the way. Your goals may change over time, but if you never set one, one thing is for sure, you will never reach it. Setting a small goal and then reaching it can be extremely exciting and fulfilling. It can allow you to stay focused and know you are on the right path. Your goals can also change over time as well as your desires. The idea is for you to get to know yourself. Experiences can help you learn what you like, what you don't, and where you want to be in all aspects of life. There is NO ONE right way to get there or do things. Remember, this is your journey and it's unique to you. This is what makes you special.

Sometimes, it takes time to figure things out and it is totally normal to be unsure of what your future will look like. That's why I say, be bold, take chances, try something new. Just, *Go for It, Girl!!!*

Chapter 9

Go for It, Girl!!!

Building resilience within the Clubhouse and Beyond!

I know growing up "Girl" can have you navigating through a lot. You are just starting those teenage years and it may feel overwhelming. There is so much that is going on in your life at this point, school, friends, family, and really learning your place in this world. I started *Go for It, Girl!!!* exactly for that reason. To give you a personal clubhouse that you can feel a part of at any point in your journey.

This is a growing up "Girl" forum where you can feel safe. I wholeheartedly would love you to join in and bring your own uniqueness to the club. I know that every decision you make during this time can affect how you feel about yourself as well as your future. What better way to meet other girls who can share and relate to some of your concerns, maybe even struggles and to be able to bring positive vibes and great energy to other girls all over the world?

I want you to feel empowered. It's ok if you feel different and don't think the world understands you. You have a platform here to be able to explore and discuss it. Your self-doubt can be turned upside down and I want to give you the tools to find your inner voice of empowerment.

You will go through a bunch of things, if you haven't already, but the most important thing is that you learn how to just *Go for It, Girl!!!*

When we go through things, it can build character, strength, and resilience. We all learn through those experiences, but if we have other girls around us that we can possibly relate to, it can make what we go through that much easier.

Building resilience is not something that is learned overnight. It is through some of life's ups and downs that we learn how to navigate obstacles while also never quieting our voices. Letting other girls know that they can *Go for It, Girl!!!* can also be a way to help you heal yourself. I know it has done remarkable things for me.

There will be bumps and bruises along the way. Life would actually be boring if we were never faced with any adversity. There is a saying, what doesn't kill you makes you stronger! Yes, a bit harsh, but you get the point. We cannot avoid the challenges that await us, but how we face them can make a world of difference.

We can go back to the beginning when I asked you if having a MAGIC PILL would allow you to handle all things "Girl," would you take it? The simple obvious answer is "YES" but the true answer would be Just *Go for It, Girl!!!* Be Bold, Take Chances, Make Moves, Be YOU!!!

Conclusion:

I hope sharing some of my growing up "Girl" experiences has given you the courage and strength to always find your way to an authentic version of your best self. There is no road map in life, and every single girl's experience will be a little bit different and unique to them as an individual.

There are things throughout this book that may be relatable and other things not as much. The important thing is to recognize that you should always have a voice, a place to feel safe, and a way to express who you are on every level.

Whether you are 12 or 20, you will be faced with decisions that only you can make. They can be as simple as wanting to spend time with a particular group of friends or choosing to study for that final exam. Either way, the power is within you to make those choices.

You are on your own unique path to greatness, you are a *Go for It, Girl!!!*

RESOURCES:

www. crisistextline. org OR: TXT HOME to 741741

www. stopbullying. gov

www. schoolsafety. gov

Last but not least:

www. goforitgirls. com

About The Author

Never did I set out to one day be the author of a book, let alone create a forum that would simultaneously be launched for everything growing up "Girl". At 46 years old, with a 30 year career in mortgages, I had already been married, divorced, then in another engagement when receiving some  devasting news that there was no possibility of ever having kids of my own. This sat heavy on my heart and I think every human being at one point in their life thinks, "What impact do or did I have in this world"? This led me to wanting to tell my story, while possibly helping even one girl navigate some of things we think we are alone with in this world. Maybe even a mom who can try and remember what it was like growing up "Girl". I am in my own empowerment and healing process and wanted to share my story while giving you the space to know its OK to just be you. I am still learning this each and every day.